Read and Play
Big Animals

by Jim Pipe

Stargazer Books

big

This bear is **big**.

3

camel

4

A **camel** is big, too.

eagle

An **eagle** is
a big bird.

7

shark

A **shark** is a big fish.

9

bison

A **bison** is big and hairy.

giraffe

12

A **giraffe** is big and tall.

rhino

14

A **rhino** is
big and wide.

15

elephant

16

An **elephant**
is bigger.

17

whale

18

A **whale** is the biggest.

19

Who am I?

rhino

elephant

giraffe

bear

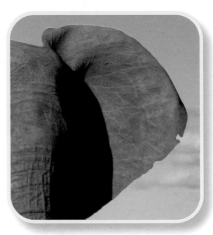

20

Match the words and pictures.

How many?

Can you count the elephants?

21

Where am I?

Bear

Lion

Shark

Camel

22 Where do these big animals live?

Index

For Parents and Teachers

Questions you could ask:

p. 2 How big is a bear? Ask the reader to guess how big the animals in the book are, e.g. a bear is almost as big as a small car—up to 11 ft (3.3 m) long and 1,400 lbs (650 kg).

p. 4 What big animals do people ride on? e.g. horses, camels, elephants. Point out the reins and saddle that help a rider to control/stay on the camel.

p. 6 What other big birds do you know? The biggest birds do not fly, e.g. ostrich, emu, but they can run very fast.

p. 8 What do sharks like to eat? Sharks eat fish and seals. But many other big animals are plant eaters: e.g. elephants, rhinos, giraffes, bison, camels.

p. 10 Can you see the bison's horns? Male bisons use their horns to fight each other. Ask readers if they know any other big animals with horns/antlers, e.g. reindeer, moose, buffalo, cattle, yak, rhinos.

p. 12 What is the longest part of a giraffe? A giraffe has a long neck to help it eat the leaves from the top of trees.

p. 16 Can you see its nose? An elephant's nose is called a trunk. It can smell, pick up and carry things, dig in the ground, or spray water or dust.

p. 18 Can you see the diver (just below the whale's mouth)? The diver shows you just how big a whale is: it is 100 ft (30 m) long (as long as 8 cars) and weighs 150 tons (the same as 2,000 people!)

Activities you could do:

• Go outside and ask readers to measure out how big the animals are, e.g. if one pace is 18 in (.5 m), bear = 6-7 paces, elephant = 18 paces, whale = 67 paces!

• Role play: ask the reader to act out their favorite big animal, e.g. elephant swinging its trunk, giant eagle flapping its wings, rhino charging.

• Plan a day for children to bring a "big animal" stuffed toy to school (dinosaurs too!). Encourage them to share information about their animals.

• Ask children to count their toes. Elephants have 4 toes on their front feet, and 3 on the back feet!

© Aladdin Books Ltd 2008

Designed and produced by
Aladdin Books Ltd

All rights reserved

Printed in the United States

Series consultant
Zoe Stillwell is an experienced preschool teacher.

First published in 2008
in the United States
by Stargazer Books
c/o The Creative Company
123 South Broad Street
P.O. Box 227
Mankato, Minnesota 56002

Photocredits:
l-left, r-right, b-bottom, t-top, c-center, m-middle
All photos on from istockphoto.com except: Cover, 1, 8-9, 14-15, 18-19, 20bl, 22bl & tr—Corbis. 6-7, 23mlb —Stockbyte. 10-11, 23mrt–US Fish and Wildlife Service. 23ml, tr, mrt & mrb—Ingram. 22bl—John Foxx.

Library of Congress Cataloging-in-Publication Data
Pipe, Jim, 1966-
    Big animals / by Jim Pipe.
       p. cm. -- (Read and play)
    Includes bibliographical references and Index.
    ISBN 978-1-59604-161-5 (alk. paper)
    1. Body size--Juvenile literature.
    2. Vertebrates--Juvenile literature.   I. Title.
QL799.3.P573 2007
590--dc22

2007007753